Lefke Automatic /
/ Destiny of Love
POEMS

Nefisa UK
Cyprus – Washington DC

Lefke Automatic / Destiny of Love

Copyright © Y. Misdaq 2011
All rights reserved. This book, or parts thereof, may not be reprinted or distributed in any form without prior permission of the author. However, those wishing to cite, discuss or use this book in any way beneficial to humankind are encouraged to contact the author.

06. Spiritual sustenance / sushi.

Published by Nefisa UK
NEFI-BK07
First Edition

ISBN 10: 0-9555024-6-2
ISBN 13: 978-0-9555024-6-0

A deemed-necessary glossary

Lefke – A small town in Northern Cyprus, home to Mawlana Shaykh Nazim Haqqani (b. April 23rd, 1922) the spiritual head of the Naqshbandi Sufi order. Lefke receives visitors of all faith traditions (and many more visitors of no faith tradition) in their thousands each year, all hoping to meet and talk with the sage Sufi master.

Mawlana – A term indicating the highest forms of respect and endearment, literally meaning, 'master' and used when talking about ones spiritual teacher or guide. In modern-day Afghanistan, Iran and Turkey the title oft-points to the well-known mystic and poet Jalal-udin Rumi (b. September 30th, 1207) however it is equally applicable to a modern-day Saint such as Shaykh Nazim (who is, incidentally, a direct descendant of Rumi on his maternal side)

Dergah – Something between a temple and a mosque. Also, in this case, the home of Mawlana Shaykh Nazim Haqqani, who lives in the separated quarters of the complex, on the second floor.

Sajjda – The act of prostration; placing ones forehead, nose and palms to the ground in complete submission.

Fajr – The dawn prayer, which is the first proscribed prayer of the day for Muslims (although many believers awaken before dawn to pray in an even more intimate part of the last third of night, for what is known as the *Tahajjud* prayer.

Salafi Ulema (read also Wahhabi) – A relatively modern group of clerics formed around the Saudi Arabian monarchy whose considerably harsh and dogmatic rhetoric, coupled with their incredible wealth and influence, has enabled them to become the default voice and mode of Muslims in both the Western and Islamic world, especially in the last century. Before its spread, Sufism was significantly less of an '–ism' and much more an integrated (and unspoken) part of everyday Islamic life, including such practices as are still practiced by Sufi groups today (chanting, spiritual dance, festive celebrations etc).

SubhanAllah, AlhamdulilLah, AllahuAkbar – incantations and praises for the one God; loosely (and decidedly inadequately) translated as *Glory be to God, Praise be to God, God is Greater*, respectively.

Bida – Literally, 'innovation!' A commonly heard condemnation used by Salafi and Wahhabi clerics who wish to label something as non-traditional, non-Islamic, and 'new' (and as such, silencing and outlawing it).

Astraghfirullah – Forgive me, God / I ask Your forgiveness.
Wa Shukran Allah – And Thank You, God.

Maghreb – Literally, 'West,' however more commonly connoting the Sunset prayer, and more generally perhaps the time of Sunset.

Vesper / Vespers – Archaic Latin term for evening prayer/s; also related to the Western, evening star.

Dhikr – Literally, 'Remembrance,' of the divine; circles of Muslims/Sufi's gather in rhythmic chanting; also alone and in silence, or by counting on rosary beads.

Hayy – 'Life.' One of the 99 Names of God, i.e. the Living.

Hu – Another name for God (literally He, God!) with endless mystical interpretations. Together with Hayy, this name is repeated in Naqshbandi Sufi Dhikr circles, and again with 'Hayy,' 'Hu' is a name 'spoken' with each breath that every human being takes with each inhalation/exhalation.

According to the Naqshbandi tradition, Hu is also the sound heard emanating at the bottom of the ocean or center of the Earth; complete bass; mysticism.

The word also has spiritual meanings that refer back to the Divine in both Sanskrit, Hebrew and ancient Egyptian. Indian mystic and musician Hazrat Inayat Khan stated that the hidden wisdom in the name 'human' was related to man's divine origin (i.e. Hu – Man).

Rahman / Rahim – [at the dawn of Islam in Arabia] *"Amongst the most striking features of the Revelation were the two Divine Names ar-Rahman and a-Rahim. The word Rahim, an intensive form of... 'merciful' was current in the sense of very merciful or boundlessly merciful. The still more intensive Rahman, for lack of any concept to fit it, had fallen into disuse. The revelation revived it in accordance with the new religion's basic need to dwell on the heights of Transcendance. Being stronger even than ar-Rahim (the All-Merciful), the Name ar-Rahman refers to the very essence or root of Mercy, that is, to the Infinite Beneficence or Goodness of God, and the Koran expressly makes it an equivalent of Allah."* [Excerpt from Martin Lings' biography of the prophet Muhammad]

Qalb – Heart

Sol – Spanish for Sun.

Khadijah – A prominent and wealthy female merchant of the Hashemite clan in Arabia born circa 555 CE. She proposed marriage to, and became the first wife of, the prophet Muhammad. She was at least 15 years his senior.

Wudu – Ablution, a ritual cleansing of the hands, arms, nose, face, hair, neck, ears and feet that all Muslims must perform before praying. It is annulled by deep sleep, intercourse and using the toilet. However, in the Naqshbandi Sufi tradition, it is encouraged to re-do ones wudu even if one loses ones temper or has unkind or foul thoughts about somebody or something. It is likewise encouraged to remain in a state of ritual purity, or, 'wudu,' at all possible times as a form of protection. The face of one who has performed Wudu glistens with luminosity.

Ka'aba – The House of God, built by Abraham and revived as a place of pilgrimage by the Prophet Muhammad, located in Mecca.

Fanaa – A term oft-used in Sufism referring to the annihilation or extinction of the lower Self / bad ego taking place whilst the physical body still lives.

Fallamanhu la illaha illalLah – 'Know that there is no God but God.' *La illaha illalLah* is one of the most commonly recited chants used in Sufi circles of dhikr, and has a very wide scope of possible interpretations and implications, such as, 'There is no truth but Truth / no reality but Reality,' etc.

Preface

This book, the sixth in the series, is a travelogue that spanned a physical, then spiritual journey. It doesn't sound all that different from the other books in the series, (for those who have been keeping up) however in many ways this was the most concentrated of all those journeys. As previously outlined in detail, in my afterword to *The Beautiful / Palace Prayers*, I had, in 2009, survived a very serious accident, made an equally serious promise to myself about becoming a better person, and then, some months after that, had a very vivid dream. The dream was of the man I went to Cyprus to see. I had never known him, and don't remember having heard his name before, and yet he appeared in the dream identical to how he appears today, a 90 year old man possessed of both incredible tenderness and a strangely magnified, father-like power of protection. When I awoke, I knew his name, and some days later, bought a ticket to Cyprus. I don't remember doing it, nor how I took the time off my considerable workload at the time. I remember only that I was in a hazy state, acting without seeming to act, doing things automatically. This man was a human being, but there was *something* about him.

As the poems project, my journey to the whole area where he lives (Northern Cyprus, a beautiful little village called Lefke) and my meeting with him were deeply profound. The place itself was suffused with his life, his energy, light and radiance, in a way that I saw nowhere else; certainly not elsewhere on the run-down, depressed Northern (Turkish) side of the Island, which seemed like a barren waste-land, some desert highways dotted with bars and night-clubs and strip-clubs, with the more suburban areas seeming equally run-down and (for an Englishman) an unpleasantly familiar feeling associated with the dreary kebab shops. And this is not to speak of the more distant Greek Cyprus, with all of its modern facilities and, it must be said, somewhat tacky aura, giving one the impression of pseudo-Europe; Belgium meets Tijuana, or a shinier Calais, with just as little soul. No, Mawlana's small village, situated between a humble mountain and a humble seaside, has a sprouting, bursting quality to its flowers, fruit and architecture that is instantly obvious (and instantly unique) to any traveler lucky enough to enter it. Lefke is (appropriately) the sort of place one has to purposefully go to; one doesn't just stumble upon it. The houses are Ottoman in the very finest tradition; not only ingeniously and ornately designed from outside and within, but warmly embracing the test of time (much less 'standing it,' passively). As I intimate in one of the poems, this magical place takes tired, hackneyed and hijacked western buzzwords like rustic and quaint, places them into a special soft machine, and turns them into qualities far more active and engaging; far more flowering.

Why, you may ask, do I attribute all of these atmospheric qualities to the man, mawlana himself? I hope I can demonstrate it with a very simple example: sometimes you go to a house and get a very good feeling about it. You feel there is light there. It might be in the middle of the busiest, ugliest city, and yet, there it is, warmth. Inevitably, this is traced back to its occupants. Not in every case, I concede, sometimes it can be traced back even further. Various Sufi masters, including mawlana, have taught that places may still retain the light, energy and intentions of its previous owners, or even of its architects or builders (this is a primary reason that mawlana encourages his numerous students in the west to gather for prayer and meditation in old Churches, Synagogues, or other places of worship when possible, for they come from a more simple time, when 'the love of God was put into every brick'. In his case, the whole of Lefke's atmosphere is *his* atmosphere. Picture yourself on a clear day in a garden. You may smell, in the distance, the scent of fresh bread being baked, or coffee. If you follow your nose (and instincts) you would eventually come to that point of origin. That kitchen. And when you got there you would have to say, "This is where the smell came from." Likewise, feeling the subtle magic in the air of Lefke, one merely has to follow ones heart-instinct, and walk towards mawlana's *dergah*, just as you see his colorful students, male and female alike equally colorful in their flowing green, red, purple, yellow shawls and loose scarves and crown-turbans, all walking towards it. The sweetly nonchalant and accepting locals all get on with their daily lives, making food that varies greatly in quality, but is all, in some way or another, truly Mediterranean. On their restaurants and windows are pictures of mawlana. Some are Muslim, some are not, all love him. And if you keep on walking, and if you are fortunate enough, you will have the chance to meet the man, and you will begin to see (there is no other word to use than 'see' although I do not refer to vision alone) that he is at the very center of it all. He is the warm scent of the village, he is the wildflowers, he is the numerous smiles, the sense of tolerance, the reality of acceptance. It all radiates from him and his incomparable presence.

There is something about meeting him which leaves every traveler feeling as though their life has been transformed in some deeply moving way. Then again, some people just laugh like mad when they are around him. I heard a story about an extremely depressed lady who went to see him. Normally he engages in conversation of some sort, but for this lady, after one look at her, he merely pointed to a spot in front of him and very sternly commanded, "Jump!" She began jumping, more and more, up and down, on the spot, until she began laughing. And then they spoke.

I myself was there as a badly-disguised journalist (recording audio interviews with people and taking photographs also, some of which you have seen) and so, made an objective account of just how many people, (some skeptics, some not, some like myself, feeling in between) had been left feeling very positive at the least and deeply changed at the more normal 'most' by their encounter/s with him. There was a German nurse whom I met one afternoon and don't think I can ever forget. She was very proper, very German, a lovely smile, still young but one of those adult-in-waiting young women. She had converted to Islam and, like me, had a guarded caution about this whole concept of Sufism, of 'holy men,' and so on. She put it in the most simple and beautifully honest way that, I think, only a German speaking English could have, "After I saw him, my heart changed".

I can speak for myself when I say that I was simply dumbfounded, astounded and enlivened by what he made me feel, not to mention what he said to me when I, on my final night, met with him. I remember I had not mentioned my music career to him, thinking it somehow inappropriate (incorrectly, I soon realized), merely describing myself as a writer and asking his advice about whether I should carry on, since I didn't seem to be having much success. He took one long, piercing look deep into me and through me, with his unspeakably strong eyes, (I still cannot tell if they are blue or green or brown, if one looks carefully, they literally seem to change from moment to moment) the look lasted for an objective fifteen seconds, feeling like a subjective decade. After this, he closed his eyes, as if he were receiving something, or listening to something, and then, some moments later, opened them again and suddenly burst out laughing. I might even call it a 'cackle,' however it was a thoroughly hearty one, which gave away his age for the first time with its raspy tone, almost reckless abandon and utter, thorough cheerfulness. *Lifefulness*. It was as if he had seen something when his eyes were closed, after his inspection of me, and now was laughing at what he had been shown,

"First you must write, and then, after that, you must sing!" Then, your success will come, he assured me. Then, for some moments, he began to sing to me. It was a strange song, wordless, although I felt in it incredible meaning. Drooping, instinctive and almost drunken sounding, although somehow, not a single note was off, and it had perfect balance and rhythm. I sang with him, instinctively for a few moments, but soon realized he was somewhere else and that my participation had nothing to do with it. His 'song' curled up and concluded in a perfect corner of quietness, ending serenely. It was as though he placed a spell of music and soul onto me. I was not the same person after that. A sense of discipline and an increased desire for soul came alive immediately after that first meeting with him. Magic, it seemed.

Before leaving I spoke to the taxi driver, the very same Emr mentioned in the first poem of this book who had first picked me up from the airport, a somewhat skeptical but open-hearted mouse, and dropped me back off at the airport on the Greek side a week or so later, a changed man. I asked him, "Has anyone ever left here angry?" I was asking because I could not believe how happy 'one old man,' had made me. I couldn't quite get myself to come to grips with the fact that he had such authority, such a seemingly powerful soul (there is no other word than soul that suffices) and most of all, that he simply was not just, 'a nice old man'. That there was something *more*. Like the best minutes of laughter in my life, or the most insistent and impossible (that is to say, potent) moments of déjà vu, this experience had poked a hole in what I thought reality was. Unlike laughter or déjà vu, this experience was not abstract, it revolved around a tangible, living person, and as such, was even more dizzying, mystifying and, ultimately, inspiring. Despite all I felt, despite the fact that I had been thoroughly convinced (and convinced by that most simplest of all things: 'seeing for myself') I still wanted to ask Emr that question. Perhaps it was on behalf of the rest of the human race, who, as an artist, I both love and feel accountable to. (Indeed, that's probably why I am sharing this book of poems.) As always, I was recording, and still have my question and his response in digital data bits. His answer was as in the poem, that he had never seen anyone leaving angry. Sometimes, he said, they may be quiet, contemplative, and yes, often they would be sad about leaving (this was certainly the case with me), but as he reminded me in his own effervescent way, "If you don't leave, you can't come back."

We arrived at the airport and I realized I had come 24 hours early. I'd never made such a huge scheduling mistake before, not once, but it made sense that I would, there in Lefke. He offered to take me back the hour and a half or so, back up North, back across the border, back to spend one more magical night in that sun-drenched, moon-filled, mystical place. But I had learned through the journey, in that village and in that *dergah*, where one's destiny seems so condensed and distilled, and through its energy and wisdom which stays with you as you leave it. Looking for the wisdom in all events is one of the most important teachings of the Naqshbandi tradition. And so I said, 'Don't worry, it feels right, this happened for a reason'. And so it did. After much wondering around, I spent the night in the baby-changing room at the well-maintained Larnaca airport. There, in that small but mercifully clean space, with a few clothes as pillow and bed spread, I put into practice one of the things I had learned of meditations. And there it was, in that baby-changing room, that I had another profoundly mystical experience; hearing once again from the smiling, aged gentleman of such boundless being, as he whispered more life-changing words into the opened ear of my consciousness.

The rest of this book charts life after the journey. Regular, working life, back in the USA, with this tariqa (or *way*) on its way to becoming a fully integrated part of my days as a television editor in Washintgon DC. I snuck away to the fire escape of the huge office building to pray many times each day. It was the first time in my life that I had maintained the discipline of praying the full 5 prayers a day on a consistent basis (and eventually this turned to much more than just 5, for when one begins to understand what worship truly is, one begins to enjoy it, and want to do it more, no struggle). As a testament to how this *way* transforms things, then, the second half of this book charts a human love that arrived unexpectedly on the doorstep of my life. It was a love that fit well with (and moved, evolving with) that larger divine love that mawlana had helped me kindle. It was not to be a wasted love, a 'just another phase' love that would burn out as those that had come before. When you are deeper, all things that you touch become deeper with you. Otherwise, you don't touch them.

In this fashion, since returning from Cyprus, I had kept my head down, worked on bettering myself as a human being, which is what Islam's spiritual core (also known more favorably to Western ears as Sufism) is all about. Nothing more, nothing else, but pure self-improvement. I wish more people could remove their blackened (or rosey, well-intentioned but totally unexamined) lenses, and see it for what it truly is. But such a path is the way of the few. The way of you.

And in accordance with mawlana's teachings, when you keep your head down, and work on bettering yourself, jewels will inevitably fall in your lap. It was thus that I met the woman to whom the second half of this book, and my life, are dedicated.

The journey never ends. As the beautiful 103 year-old Japanese man said at the end of Akira Kurosawa's final cinematic masterpiece, *Dreams*, "Some say life is hard, but that's just talk. In fact, it's good to be alive. It's exciting."

Yusuf Misdaq,
Salima, Malawi,
December 25th, 2011

Lefke Automatic
&
Destiny of Love

Lefke Automatic [January 2010]

The airport driver is called 'Emr' or 'Omar'

He says: "Everybody always win in Lefke"

He says: "Never I have seen anybody coming back angry from Mawlana, in 8 years driving people."

He says: "Nobody lose when they coming to Lefke."

Written in front of Mawlana

Green Hearts

Go Strong

Love Gardens

Bird Song

Tole,
Pearl,
Preesus,
Majestus

You have been called here
Collect yourself

.Your bags have already been packed.
The road has been written

Regard your
Opened palms
At dawn
They are meant to be here
Before you
Basking in the blue
Bath of prayer
Bubbles
 Music
Bubbles
Faith/Breathing in real time

Making every moment wet
With electricity

Flashing oranges &
Intricate twigskies
Will be your gifts
Each time you blink

<u>Welcome!</u>

Lefke is not rustic
It is not romantic
It is not charming

It is the deepest essence
Of what these words attempt to point to.

It is a place on this Earth
Suspended in Heaven-Time

It is the smallest whiff of
Eternity

Blown softly

From the blessed man

Who sits comfortably all day in a chair
At the heart of the diving-board dergah

"Deliver us to Unity Oceans! Please!"

Men of serious stuff spend the last 1/3 of the night in prayer. They are beautiful, handsome creatures of the moon and its light. They are praying in what seems like automatic-motion; relentless. Their drive is a serious selfishness to be the best of their best-selves. They will not quit. They will not fail. By the black light and the still movements, by the silent grace and blurry faces, shall they poke their souls through the cloud-cover.

They shall begin on the road to eternity, which is paved with discipline's disciples (as well as good intentions). This road has an ocean on both sides. The wave-ends encroach onto the road, touching and teaching the serious Lovers, tickling their toes and enticing them to keep on with this magic, balanced lifestyle.

This midnight of dreaming motions.

They are encouraged by the sight of scattered sajjda bodies upon huge boulders, some of which rise out from just beyond the shallows of the ocean, and others from the sands of the shore. Believers are hunched over on these boulders, prostrate, heads all facing the same direction. They are perched perfectly on the black rocks like cats or hawks, with a thin tide trickling beneath them and an Ocean waiting 'fore them.

Intelligent, humble creatures of the oncoming daylight.

Delicious! / Village Life

After Fajr prayers in the dergah
Go for a victory-lap outside somewhere
And watch the sun
Really rise.

That spreading
Sobering blessing
Is a personal gift
To You
From God

And when you come to face the **orange groves**
You will see a low-hanging
Exotic invitation

Jump up!
Grab happiness!

Two other Mosques

I saw two other Mosques in Lefke.
They seemed official.

One had a Turkish flag on it
The other had posted 'opening times'.

One had seven believers for the afternoon prayer
The other was constantly locked and empty

This dergah is fit to explode
With all of the international atoms
Packed with love inside of it

A brief, desperate message from the fading Salafi ulema

It is *bida* to harmoniously chant *SubhanAllah*
                                    AlhamdulIllah
                                    Allahu Akbar

BIDA!

It is bida to shake the hands of your brothers and stand in a circle-bond of unbreakable unity after prayers.

BIDA!

It is BIDA to believe in your dreams
Or interpret them!
Especially if you dream about Mawlana
Or another person who has devoted their life to God
And isn't one of **us**.
 (Who are *we*, you ask?
   Shaded in luxurious saudi-mystery and
   Unknowable
   To the working masses)

BIDA!!!

Stop all this child's play!
All this dance
All this laughter

All this broad-mindedness and
CHEERFULNESS!

Enough now!
Go back to being
Stern-faced and rigid!

Return to your suspicious ways and
JUDGE!
JUDGE!
JUDGE, with *our* standards!

Don't let love win, damn you!
Wake up!

Can't you see???

It's a cloudy day!!!

ACT LIKE IT!!!

When Mawlana looks at you

It is *really* happening

And it is a dream

Never so Close

The purple bolt chords come
Cutting the sky down
And the God is infused, re-
Vamped and amped in you
For some small bubbling days
Of elocution and HD dreams and
Destiny never was so frozen
Into a sunny road that you can **see**

      Is not unknown
      Or fruitless

Perhaps the good future will never again feel
So close
      So attainable as it does here.

Or, softly,
Perhaps this realization can never go black
To chasms of uncertainty
Depressions of disbelief
The loveless indiscipline which
Leads to disaster

There, once before
I was drowned and
Made to be
Here.

Very softly then,
Perhaps I will never be so far gone again.

    Astaghfirullah . Astaghfirullah . Astaghfirullah.

    Wa Shukran Allah

Attraction

Here I meet a new family.

All kinds of funky and free-flying
Atoms come magnetized
Towards Mawlana's melting pot

And whilst here, some of them
Attract one another's souls also

Everyone is a part of the same rosary
But some beads like to be really close
Some beads want to always sit next to each other.

Say nothing //
Nothing needs anything //
Be the droplet //
Drop everything //

Back to the fake real world [February 2010]

Nonsense ("What is that foolishness?")

In Larnaca airport
There are 9 TV's which join to make one huge TV.

Yes, *TV's!*
In just one week I had forgotten all about those
                                                silly
                                                    things.

On the screen there is a TV show, a magician.
He is a ridiculous man in a tuxedo
Making a big show of himself.
The format is so ridiculously cliché, but not here.
He is young and not unattractive
So perhaps he doesn't realise he is ridiculous.
The Greek-Cypriot studio audience are SILENT!
He is putting a sword very carefully down his throat.
With drum rolls and suspense music!
He has to do it very carefully.
Inch by deliberate inch.
Otherwise he might lose his head.

When he has done this
And the hilt of the sword is sticking out of his
Forced grin mouth
The studio audience release their dramatic, earnest
Mediterranean tension
And they CLAP! Wide eyed!

But he is not finished!
He is handed a white balancing pole,

Which he places on his chin
Just below the sword and the foolish looking
                                open mouth.
Then, two smiling assistants wearing lots of glitter
Hang miniature televisions onto either end of the balancing pole.

So, now he has not only swallowed a sword
But is balancing two televisions at the same time.

He holds his arms out, theatrically
As if he has just climbed Everest
And they clap again, harder.

The director cuts to a vivacious audience member
Who is a girlfriend of a man beside her.
She is much more enthusiastic than her partner
And as she claps, she urges him to be more enthusiastic
With a subtle leaning-in, and
A mere glance.
He claps too, but slightly slower.
He nods his head, for her sake, forces a smile
As if to say that he knows he *should* be impressed by
All this nonsense
As if admitting, silently
Begrudgingly
That this is as good as it's ever going to get.

(*Nonsense!*)

<u>Kind old man with no family wandering New York City streets with slippers in Winter / The cold gets in.</u>

Crime uncaring
Coldness crime
Candles of confusion
Burning backwards

Prizes loaded
Happiness hangs
Heavy happiness
Whoever had it?

Whoever came first?
Creative contracts
Calm cardiologists
Hearts attacked

Whole under threat
Particles run
Rage is wet
Dripping angry sun

Dropping dung and diamonds
Just the angle of eyes
Just the Season of soul
Is what determines a prize

Cries
        Uncaring
Coldness cries

Catalogued courage

Give us
        Gold & Freedom

Give us family footsteps

Mothers and fingers, filling
Care with convoys
Of Love that lingers

Pungent
Still in the air for years long

Rolling
In through our lives like old songs
Like old songs
Like old songs
Stay for sunset

Stay for sunrise
Stay 'til I'm Gold and I close my eyes

Stay for sunrise
Stay for sunrise
Stay with my neck and my heart's the prize

My gmail account and most of it's contents are ego
My thoughts are ego
My 'kindness' is ego
My 'sweetness' is ego
My 'love' is ego
My desires are ego

<u>Me go now</u>

Slow
Go slow into the warm dark pasture

Envelops you and surrounds you
Its texture is smooth and velvet
.Space without stars.

Soft
Be soft
In the tickling night
The glint of light is a loudest whisper

Vesper, vesper,
Maghreb, vespers
Vapours swarm as a storm of
Openings

Perishings

Peaces

Latitudes

Openings

Bead by beautiful bead
Dhikr'd head-first into Heaven

<u>Blueberries before Sunset</u>

Reward

If you are willing to be a **True Lover**
That the other one will consent to be loved

Older

Faces fade away and become flowers that do not die
In the eternity of *life*
When it is seen through spirit

It is hard for me to accept
That I will not be a young man anymore
It is hard for me to accept
These pains that take longer to
Drain away

If only I can live in the falls of Eternity
It will not be hard to accept

If only I can remain there
In Spirit-wind
For longer than a few
Snatching moments

Hayy! Hai! High!

Hu!   (who?) ... <u>HU</u>!

. Yes . Yes . Yes !

endlessly, endlessly,

<u>**yes**</u>

Longing and holding and
Needing and having and
Empty-handed happy-ness!

To be a Prince/ss of Zero
In a Royal Kingdom of blessed
Nothingness
Where your name is called
With honour by some angel nobody can see
And you are almost invisible to the people of this

   Money-laundering world
   Of wasted waiters
   And self-serving slaves
   Who would have you believe
   That you need a trick up your sleeve
   Or some outer, shiny garment
   To show off
   As evidence that you are original and
   Different!

When in your eyes, already, is the glint of the prize:

The Crown of crescent and full-moon.
The Lord of *sol*
And what *sol* shines upon
The throne over space and stars
Whose first blessed steps
Are in your drippingful heart

Drown yourself in God.

Plunge your head into *Rahman*

Bathe your *Qalb* in *Rahim*

Be all and together

(Endlessly, oceans)

I'm ready to fall for You at any moment
It used to be that only evening prayers made me tearful
Now I'm falling apart and spilling out of myself
5 times a day
Even in the middle of the sober afternoon

Gently disintegrating in sajjda
Meekly retreating
Trying to shrink even more
And <u>perhaps</u>
Beginning to understand <u>something</u> of what

   Our beloved
                felt, when he ran home to Khadijah

And cried,

      "Cover me!"

Let us be raised to the Prophet
Like a Jewel   // In him
Let us become Weeping Willows
Sleeping pillows
Keeping halos
And deepening zero's

This life without him inside of us is like
Fast food alone in a loveless home

We need a lover to love and one
Who would love us all the way to the Highwards
Highness
Highland, No-land
Upwards

Forever and a heart that is
Shooting star
That is
Blazing sparks
In a path of fire
In a flame of life
With a gust of yes
And a freshness air
As the heart-soul nests
In a breath
In a place
In a changing garden
Going for a second in a
Rosebush, ardent

Farragut West Metro Station at a rush-hour

All these people pouring out of the transport system are blood from a wound that does not stop gushing.

All these people falling into the station are floating Antidotes

Aimed kisses
On their way, blindly
To balm the world.

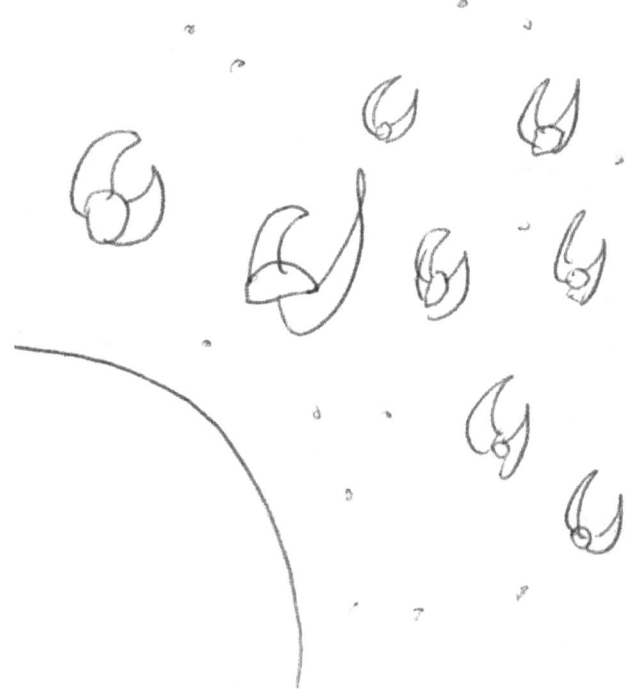

If you understand the rapidly decaying nature of this

>   Bottom-line'd
>   Mercy-blasting
>   Cloud-busting
>   Promise-breaking
>   'world'

Then <u>smoking cigarettes</u> suddenly makes perfect sense.

But let's not be too quick to celebrate pessimism.

If you are able to accept those harsh facts of life
Without turning them into excuses
And then relegate them so that the improvement of
Your character becomes your target, your
   Paramount-peak

Then hope, preservation and walks in the park
Inevitably begin to make perfect sense.

On beautiful Spring days in parks, you tend not to see smokers. Smokers smoke because they cannot bring themselves to fully believe in Spring. Not all the way. They cannot come to terms with the fact that life contains infinitely more blessings than hardships. They need something bad to hold on to.

<u>Smokers hijacked as exemplars</u>

I still want this world too much

I still turn my head when I sense a disruption
Sense a new face coming
From the corner of my eye.
Hoping it for a flower
Silently yearning for exoticism

Gold

"She's of Gold."

I still want this world more

I do not leap towards *wudu* the way I leap towards life
And blue skies

I do not *rush to prayer*.

And when I'm hungry, I want to eat

And when I eat
I strengthen the bond
The binding bond
Between material and man

I still look at my beautiful mirror
With absent eyes
Forgetting everything
In a low lulling admiration

Of the features I was given
Which could have been harshly out of proportion

But are not

What to make of it all?
What to make of my hands?
My voicebox?
My skin and eyes?

Only to say that when I awaken for prayers at dawn
I am more beautiful

Only to say that when I fast
I am more satiated

Annihilation is easy to talk about
So let us stop talking about it.

What makes us lazy?
What makes us accept less and
Trick ourselves that it's good?

Where does laziness come from?
Which abyss?
What lack gives it space to be
And yield a sway over us?

Why have we lost the desire to be great?
When did idiots begin to equate
Greatness with self-righteousness?
When did it become unfashionable
To be great?

Where is the leak in our society
That we are all so pleased with ourselves
To be smart and quick
And speaking all the time?

Wherefore a hushed magnificence?
Wherefore a *magnificence*?
Clouds from above
The size of continents
Yet lighter than grace.

Do you feel it in your veins?

What do you feel?

Destiny of Love [Spring, 2010]

Visions of Her (Don't blame it on the City)

There is, in you
A fine patience for
Rivers
   Still
       as you (certainly)
Surge t'ward me.

And in I
– A recently done storm –
My vapours run
Wildly still, sometimes
Straying and searching
From the concrete cuts.

It is the fact that I'm here
In this city of non-believers
That I am not a river.
That I have not the stillness
Not the vision to see you.

Even on this cheap tissue paper
Flowers are embossed.

We can't live without
Ornaments and choirs and
Floral scenes and
Fantastic arrangements

We can't function well if nothing matters
If you die when you die
And if all the colorful traditions
Are just 'subjects' to study
Which only a fool would *believe* in.

Corporeal Crescent carries
Waves that wander hither
'pon the upperdown clouds
And the drifting darlings

Do you foresee the forever-a
Fountain? Far upon the Isle
So long and misty

Can you behold the eternity
Moment? Lost in a scene that you
Will remember

Give up the hand-held things for current
Creation is a thought-pulse
Peace away.

Flood up the heart for a risky deep-dive
A risk-free bee-hive
The sting of a bubble-dream

<u>Do you want Happiness, or not?</u>

Comemama seeme
Seeme climb the mountain!
Seeme run so fast
Seeme try an' impress you.

Here, baba, look
Look the man I been
Look the sweat I sung
Comesee the things I done.

But what I do when no
Body is looking? When no
Body is clapping? When no
Body reacting?

Where I go when I'm all alone?
When the stillness-silence
Is a sinking stone?

Freedom Fitra / The Breast of Flower-soul

Step onto the escalator
And glide
Soft travel inside takes you to inner
Treedoms.

Go slow!

        Slower!

Until the outer rims of your iris are as black as the pupil
Until you are degenerated from professor back down to undergrad

And your starkle
Thunder
Once again awaits a direction

Walk into the darkest center of a rose
Navigating the shady
Meaning-folds

Migrate as atoms

Back to your seed-self

And remain there
   In your own secret

Oh, my Darling!

"Oh, my darling!
You are sooo beautiful !
I am for you and only you !

Therefore:
Let us buy a new Mercedez-Benz
And a big house!
A thousand thousands!

Oh, my darling
You are everything to me!
Therefore: you must wear the latest fashions
So that everybody can see you and
Think of me.

Oh, my darling!
Let us kiss and cuddle!
And as we do so
Broadcast ourselves via Twitter
And change our status to:
"Kissing and cuddling!"
Let the world see our love
And *validate* it
With *comments*, oh my darling!

We don't need
                Anything!
Except each other!

And the right style of cool friends
And a satellite dish
And a new garage
And a walk-in closet
And an electronic shoe-buffer
With a built-in sensor
And precious alone time with girl friends
And, definitely, a *huge bed*
So that we wake up
Far   apart

So that you have your things
And I have mine
And we grow more
And more
And more
Bonded to this delicious world, oh,
My darling

So that we end up as two pieces of a compass
Ripped apart
And flung to distant places
With only a faint memory
Of each other, by the
Time
    We're old,
             oh,
My *Darling.*"

<u>O my love</u>

Let's walk this line of courage together
We can make it together
Tangled in sweaty hand & heart
Two triangles, twinned and total'd
Turning towards the rising horizon

You and I to form a teamwork
Of dreamblocks
Upon this desolate scattering
Of concrete need
Of deep, deep want.

Let's kiss this broken world morning
                                            together.

We can make it together.

Turn to me and try
Push for me!
As if you were my mother in labour
Let your world depend upon me…
Mine: on your kindness.
All of the whole of me, resting upon
Your kindness
Me milking it, and – hopefully –
Giving something that I'm unaware of
To you, as your milk.

And for some time
–Some years, if we are lucky–
Let us lick, drink and
Swallow one another.

Pieces and whole
Whole and pieces

For all the love that we need
For all the love that is our due

The Human Race (Song of her #1)

See flowers in my eyelids
Purple, and they move
Oozing into circles
I'm lying in my bed

The feeling flows as feelings do
Through the cracks of dark
I feel it when I think of you
And all the things I want to start

Ohh, oh, oh, ...
Hearts keep flooding and I am the human race.
Ohh, oh, oh, ...
Hearts keeps running and the feelings on my face.

I wanna start some kind of bush-fire
I want to spark it in your soul
I wanna turn your heart to loving me
I'm a black dusty chunk of coal

I'm a gold-dust daddy deliverer
If you only would say yes
I'm a skinny self-doubting shiverer
Unless you love me like I'm the best

Ohh, oh, oh, ...
Hearts keep flooding and I am the human race.
Ohh, oh, oh, ...
Hearts keeps running and the feelings on my face.

Give your time and space to me
Give me what I need to live
For all the things that you'll be giving me
There'll be things I'll unconsciously give

You are a jewel that I will hold you
On my shoulders to face the sun
You are a perfect dream, I told you
Just allow me to come undone

Ohh, oh, oh, ...
Hearts keep flooding and I am the human race.
Ohh, oh, oh, ...
Hearts keeps running and the feelings on my face.

Inspiration & Works of Art
==========================

Manner

My majestic moment
Means everything to me.

I stay alone when I know it is coming and
Have begun to feel
When God is about to
Carve me open
And let free an eloquence
That was held in me.

Some fluttering group of
Doves is released
Without ceremony or onlookers.
Only for their pleasure
(and mine on their behalf)

The Doves emboss into the sky

Stamps / Poems

To glint for all time
Hereafter.

Suddenly it's Springtime / Tender Springtime

Why again, so tender?
Why, amidst natural beauty
Flourishing upon the people so needy
Why do I quiver again
As the perfect warmth forgives
And holds my soul?

This year
This Spring
My answer is deeper than it was last:

It is the fear of dreams being realized.
The unworthiness one feels when a wish is granted.

Do they feel it too?
I cannot say.
Some still have Winter-faces
And haven't yet let it in.
Perhaps their lives are always
Winter lives.
Grinding.
          I only know me.

And I feel so shy before the Bringer of Spring.

This is what I longed for
Throughout the darker time
Without ever saying or thinking it explicitly

I know undeniably that
This is the gift I wished for.

But when it is here
Aliving me and
A reality
I get scared.
With weak knees

Lightness inside
     me

hollow.

Can't be confident in my body self
Can't walk around taking it all in
As if it were just 'nice weather'
And not a perfect symbol
Of Mercy
Kindness

I can't walk around as though I deserve it
Have earned it

It is too beautiful

Too much beauty
That it cannot be compared to the
Sadness of Winter in some
Yin-Yang / proportionate / correlation of equality.
This is too beautiful for that.

And so then…

Heaven?

PARADISE?

All this wondrousness being just a
                                        whisper?

                                        just a hint?

How, then, could I not spend the rest of my life in   Royalty Sajjda?

Head bowed down in worship to the Lord of Life.

How, now, can I *not*?

Fridges. Falas. Far-reaching. Carunda.

Magnificent phones connect us
Magnificent feathers connect us
Floaters in the union-sky of You.

YOU ! ?

Your nature , is so knowable
So obviously kind
Understandable.

But you only allow for it to feel so
It's another Mercy you give
Like the first morning's
Unconscious waking-breath
      Unconstricted, allowed
         Wide open like a flute-note

You pierce through the air
You are the air
You are my consciousness of what you are

      Y'are my pen.
      Y'are my fingers

My thousand of dark hairs
My six of white

My calm in the daybreeze
My star of the night.

Where do I go, but for reaching and stretching?
What do I do, but for thanking while resting?

Let go of poetry; poetry's trying
Lie-still in sun; the grass is for *lying*

Smoke, Spirit, Stations, Spaces

Believe in more than cars and your material world will crash

With spirit years, your yolk will smoke up like curling
Roses in the night where evolution happens.
Through slow years, you will parallel park into a perfect spot
of spirituality which is
Your destined station

A place is reserved for you in this life, too
And is waiting for you

Like the perfect partner
Who is not your end
But your means
To that parking space
                      // starting place

Collector of Creation
Sweeps us through and through.

The road ahead is easy!
The road ahead is Reality!
What do you need
But for clean water
And a faithful heart?

My sister-heart, distant and lovely

Circumambulates the Ka'aba
Whilst I, in an empty DC elevator
Robot-rising to the 6th floor
Spin round on the spot like a madman
A madman / Muslim
(Marriage made in Heaven)
And chant Allah Hu Akbar 7 times
Before the doors open

Before the doors open.

For me: work

For her: endless pleasement
Deep spiritual sleep

The empty holiday feeling

Open and spare for use

Open for Him to make you move in destiny ways
For destiny days
Docile and daring
Dreaming and driving
       in your mind
Pink plans forming
Firm and gentle
Notions and whispers
True as clouds
To be implemented upon your return

Return to higher cycles
Happiness cycles
Drunken, gentle, loving circles.

Dhikr.

The Master

The Master of the Universe
Is.

He is the Allower.

And He allows you to finish this sentence.

Did you finish it?

Waaw!

After Dua Kumayl

Care. Frill. Partition. Turnstile. Relayed. Rar. Garden. Parade.

I come to you as empty
Oh Lord

And empty as shaking
And shaking as weak

Here is my peak

Here, perfection

Where I am released of their fingers
Fallen of their fantasies, returning
First from my funeral

Freedom'd in a first-stage fanaa.

Fire for me.
Your Fire for me is
All.

Burn me off me
Remove the self-cyst
That cancerous
Selfishness
Size of a large pea
Which foolishly
Controls me.

Give me no senses
   No senses
No sense
No sentences

Grant me
Emptiness and
Vessels to be
Voyaging in
T'ward You

Give me open-ness
And spaces for
Imagination trills to
Chord You.

<u>Species high</u>

Respond to the birds which call upon you from the rain
When it falls at night
And when they fall into you at night

Respond to the colorful shawls and headscarves of
Beautified believers
That simultaneously say
Look at beauty! And
Don't look!

Respond inside
Your flutes respond
With music by breathing
And the rushing, racing blood
Which is bleeding just by breeding
Inside of your productive, planetary personage.

Peerless and without equal among your race of
Servants and slaves
You are not going to be put down or
Bettered by any other
Except in piety.

He, the King of Dazzelement
The Trust of Yes
The Eternally expanding Lord of
Everything

He cannot be held anywhere

Or contained in any way
Except in your heart.

You, reading this:

Only your heart
Can hold Him.

Openitunity

The first fold is to accept one woman.

You close your eyes to all of the other forms and manifestations and you say: "This is the one I will Honour. This is the jewel I choose."

You are tired, and realize your limitations:
You cannot have all of the jewels.
The world is too large.

You are energized and see infinity in her soul.
You want your journey to the Infinite One to be
With her.

The first opening is when He grants you one woman.

Beginning

Pretty flirting vision of piety
You have either been ordained to pass me by
Or please me closely.
I have no say in the matter.

And yet I am greedy.
And would not wish to become a
Momentary admirer
Gleaning only seconds of salvation from you.

Those certain birds who are in love with
Flight, and are lite
Spend every moment they can
.In. the sky.

Inside its holding harvest.

Having it   ///   Had.

.Yad.

My hand wishes to sink through your corporeal
Melt into your metaphysical vessel
Become a train conductor
From the land of you
Speaking the language of you
In the dialect of you

Who calls out loudly through the carriage
Through the sinking pleasure ship,

"All aboard!"

He calls back outwards
To external Yusuf
Making sure that I understand
That if I want what I say I want
I am going to have to step in fully
Both feet
And leave behind many of the things from my country

That is what conductors are here for
To let you know when you are leaving one station
For another.
To warn. To congratulate

By simply announcing

"Next stop, …… *Love.*"

I sit down by the window like a freshly orphaned child as the train pulls away and the views that I know begin to roll and go. I hold onto my suitcase with fear and happiness. It contains only the things that we may enjoy together.

Yellow is the colour of Gold
Gardens are the heart of You
Let's stay in touch 'til we're old
I want to see the varying hues.

※

Hold my hand
It is an instrument that needs
Goodness to guide it.

I need you
To get me to
Him.
You are an instrument too.
Yet you have fur
And you pur

Stir me vigorously
For many years
Allow me to climb
The mountain of fears

Keep me close
Keep us both close to Him
(Stars in the the clouds
Under shrouds, stay twinkling)

Just Do it

Moments come and fill with liquid
Drown and
Leave you.

What are you going to do?

You will drown too.

And when you do
The moments will be irrelevant
The feet and fingers will stale
And the heart will freeze

What will you do?

The conversation will dry up
The juice will be diluted
With tap water
.No true tastes.
Nothing but tablets
Toilets
and time-killing.

When you ask me what
I will say what Mawlana said:

JUMP!

JUMP!

And find your feet again
And feel your fingers and
Breathe your heart and
Eagle your arms and
Open your neck and
Nourish your face and feel
God is Sun and
God is One.

Song of her # 2

Are you a diamond-studded library?
Are you a ruby-studded star?
Are you a universal theory?
Are you a woman who is far?

Are you a lover, of the beaches?
Are you a giver, from inside?
Are you a dream of rosey peaches?
Are you a strong unending ride?

Where is the tapestry of time?
What does it look like when complete?
What kind of role will you play for me?
What kind of cycle will you be?

Will you propose with YES-ing eyelids?
Will you propose with your consent?
Will you give in to me with beamers?
Will you empower me with dents?

Will you consent to be an *agitant*?
Will you <u>not</u> let me be smooth?
Will you get all up in my face, yo?
Will you give me things to prove?

I don't want no satisfaction
I don't want no saline drip
I just want some human action
I just want some cheeky lip

Come sing a song
Come do it well for me
Don't try hard just try to be

Come sing a song
Come sing it beautif'ly
Come make my ♥ feel fully free

Automatic Transmission [Spring-May 2010]

Under the Nineveh sky
One eye and a pistachio shell
In my hand, so I can fly
See your eyes
Like fish in a school
   Water run down like waterfall pool
Your forehead is smiling
And I don't know how
All I know is these are the thoughts I think <u>now</u>
All I see is how my face looks <u>today</u>
And all I feel here is that I want to stay
This café, home, this country, life
But if I'm gonna stay I'll need to find me a wife
The pipes get blocked if the water don't run
The water don't run if you ain't having fun
You can't have fun 'til you fall down to funerals
Dumbed by darkness
Stunned by hardness
Somehow endure it to your
Open-Arms-ness
Your freedom harness
Your discipline dances
Your trillion chances…
Your far-ness, far-ness

Closeness, closeness
We are all slaves lackin' focus, focus
We want love, lines, overdoses
We are the race of Heart-Lotus-Lotus
Roses, water, with the weight of Moses
The spirit is a wind that nobody opposes

When we feel it strong then we know what we owe is
A life on knees saying:

"I am nothing"

Let-me-be a thing,
   -me-be connected to the essence
Searching for the source, all I see is salad dressing

Mustard-men –full-'a-gas– sneeze and breezy
Stresspots calling the scapegoats the black ones
Ketchup queens who think it's all so easy
Lamb-chop lovers 'til the heart attack comes

Don't wait 'til your breakdown comes to believe
Break yourself down right now to breathe

Retro

Cancel the night out
Where we would only have
Relented into an evening of war stories
And bland consoling of each other
For the repeated mistakes we make.

For tonight
Is a night to
Dive in deeply by candlelight
With no digital presence
No distracting elements

Just...

(Can you believe it?)

You!
         And
   Candles!

And
         Dark!   And

   Thoughts.

Who would have thought life could be
This retro!?!
And evolutionary.

Where I feel
I peeled back some new
Layers to my Soul

And my veins got calm
And my heart got gold
And my body felt still

And my eyes didn't burn
And my voice didn't burst
And my skin felt real.

Dear Mawlana:
For Terrance Malick & Catherine Bush

It has been three months since I saw you
And I feel my heart drying.
You bring me closer to God
Like a pillow brings me closer to sleep.
But now this world of bins and biscuits
Feels real; less ludicrous
This world of toilets and masks
And deadlines and tasks
Seems realistic.

How deep am I dreaming?
How dark are my delusions?

What is from Him?
And what is from me?

Help me to drown my heart once again
Help me to mess up the perfect practical
Painting by throwing a tin of
WHITE onto it.
Help me to *take my shoes off*
And throw them in the lake!

Help me to the freedom of spirit
Where my intellect can make itself useful
For a change

And design a ladder of my own
Style and speed

Custom'd for my ways
To help me in my days

To be beautiful here
But closer to there

*(I don't know what's good for me
I don't know what's good for me...)*

<u>In a small teeny-weeny tidy sushi restaurant</u>

YOU CAN'T TAME MY HEART!!! **NO ! ! !**

IT RUNS ON FIRE!! !
SOME KIND OF FIRE! ! !

And you won't match it –

You won't know how deep it
B　U　R　N　S　!

Except by watching me, spirit, as I
turn and turn.

Divide the world up into little tidy bits of sushi
If you want.

Make rituals out of eating and shitting
If you want.

You're the one with the world on your side
Not me.

And God knows this globe is the
Best way to be free.

God knows this grounded heart
Is the thing to put your ears onto.

Listen to the oncoming convoys
of creation

Listen to the circle-thumps that
Signify birth and soul-star unification

Stop looking for orgasms everywhere you go.
Stop looking for fireworks and rainbows; go slow.

Earn it.
Starve yourself.
Earn it.
Deserve it.

One day you will have heaven in your belly. You will be pregnant with the future and giving birth at every wave that spills upon you, spilling seeds of now all down upon your toes where it tickles and where it goes when you travel and grows.

Where you stop?

No
Body
Knows

Where you pop?
God is your destiny.

God is your destination

...Is your heart
Is your aim
Is your agent of change

   –And subtle phasing
     Between the changes–

Seasons sun with their
Expected pages

Nothing is new
Just true
Through ages

The Submission

Chisel away
At a buzzing sound

Mould like clay
The Ocean

Fall in love
With a dead man

Give your spirit
To a windy flag

Agree to disagree with
Swaying branches
Saying
Rustling leaves

Accept the argument of
Overcast cloudsky
When it never leaves.

As a fabricated one
You are as made up as concrete
And this should not bother you unduly

Any more than a businessman sneezing in your face
Would

Or a child vomiting on you
Would

Or a person you love speaking unkindly
And stinging.

The marvelous monstrosities
Unmerge through moving millennia to show you all
One.

All One.   All won over by one
Infinite One.

Fallamanhu la illaha illalLah

Fountain of Water

Atop the fountain
It bubbles and
Tumbles over itself
Spills inside itself

Constantly reaching and
Failing, continuously

Forever failing
Insufficient always

Trying!

Forever young
Because
Trying!

Here lies a life lived well.

Beauty drops in all forms and at all times
It comes into your life and loves you or
Wounds you

It is always trickling down upon your forehead
Whether you're happy to receive it like a farmer or
Angry and fleeing like a city-dweller
It will keep on falling on your forehead.

If you are riding a motorbike
With a helmet
And thick gloves
And a covering scarf
And sunglasses
And contact lenses
And a computer screen on the lens of your visor
And internet whilst you drive
And ipod playlists barking in your ear
You will not block any of it out.

It will still be pounding its chest of
Tree and wood-hearts
And sky, and saying, "Here!
HERE AND CREATED!"

A swarm of low-flying birds will catch up with you
On your motorbike
As you speed on towards ambition.
You see them by your side for a few moments

Mad birds,
Smiling at you whilst backstroking the air at
55 mph.

You will know instinctively that they could overtake you if
they wanted to
But instead they make a sudden dash
     Sideways
                            Diagonally out to some random
     destination

     Not parallel with the highway and its sweating
Straight lines
But,

    Foof!

Shot straight up into a corner that you'd never know existed
Until they reached it.

Some fresh interplay of leaves and angles
That disqualifies all physics and
Drums home the fact that
All the creatures on this planet run on
Differing star-charts.

<u>Life is bigger than Beauty</u>
<u>(It has a divine Intelligence)</u>

Whoever is willing to be a True Lover
Will win

The author sitting before Mawlana Shaykh Nazim al-Haqqani
Lefke, Cyprus, 2010

Also available & coming soon from Yusuf Misdaq

The Beautiful / Palace Prayers (Poetry)	NEFI-BK06
The Butterfly Gate (Poetry)	NEFI-BK05
Spilling Kingdoms (Poetry)	NEFI-BK04
Into Solidity (Poetry)	NEFI-BK03
Brighton Streets (Poetry)	NEFI-BK02
Pieces of a Paki (Novel)	NEFI-BK01
[No Title] (Documentary)	NEFI-CD03
Maghreb, Isha & Space (Music, LP)	NEFI-CD03
Flowers & Trees (Music, LP)	NEFI-CD02
From a Western Box (Music, LP)	NEFI-CD01

Narayan (Novel)
The Steep Ascent (Novel)

www.ingramcontent.com/pod-product-compliance
Lightning Source LLC
Chambersburg PA
CBHW032047040426
42449CB00007B/1012